Introduction to Growing Onions and Leeks Easily in Your Garden

Gardening Series

Dueep Jyot Singh

Mendon Cottage Books

JD-Biz Publishing

All Rights Reserved.

No part of this publication may be reproduced in any form or by any means, including scanning, photocopying, or otherwise without prior written permission from JD-Biz Corp Copyright © 2015

All Images Licensed by Fotolia and 123RF.

Disclaimer

The information is this book is provided for informational purposes only. It is not intended to be used and medical advice or a substitute for proper medical treatment by a qualified health care provider. The information is believed to be accurate as presented based on research by the author.

The contents have not been evaluated by the U.S. Food and Drug Administration or any other Government or Health Organization and the contents in this book are not to be used to treat cure or prevent disease.

The author or publisher is not responsible for the use or safety of any diet, procedure or treatment mentioned in this book. The author or publisher is not responsible for errors or omissions that may exist.

Warning

The Book is for informational purposes only and before taking on any diet, treatment or medical procedure, it is recommended to consult with your primary health care provider.

Our books are available at

1. Amazon.com
2. Barnes and Noble
3. Itunes
4. Kobo
5. Smashwords
6. Google Play Books

Table of Contents

Introduction 5

Garlic 9

    Harvesting 13

    Health Benefits of Garlic 15

    Weight Loss through Garlic 16

    Antiviral and Antibacterial 18

    Skin Protector 20

    Garlic for Your Liver 22

    Blood Sugar Reduction 23

    Cholesterol Reduction 23

Onions 25

    Soil Preparation for Onions 26

    Seed Propagation 29

    Planting 29

    Thinning 31

    Proper cultivation of Onions 31

    Harvesting 33

    To Top or Not to Top 34

    Storage 35

Chives 37

Shallots 40

    Growing Shallots 40

    Harvest 42

    Growing shallots for Bulbs 44

Leeks 46

    Leek Propagation 47

Conclusion 49

Author Bio 51

Publisher 62

Introduction

Just do a little bit of mental globetrotting and think of all the cuisines in the world. There is absolutely no cuisine anywhere in the world, which has not used a member of the Allium family in some form or the other to make delicious fare for hungry families, down the ages.

Start them young…

Just imagine a world where we cook vegetables mixed with herbs and spices. But imagine if he did not know about this extra herbal flavoring in the shape of onions, garlic, shallots, chives and leeks. Thanks to the antibacterial qualities of garlic and onions, how many people have been saved from diseases and germs, down the ages? One cannot visualize the number thanks to the varied benefits of these particular herbs.

I remember somebody ancient telling me when I was a child that in her time, anybody who seemed to be lethargic and without energy was immediately told to go into the garden, pluck a fresh onion, and chew upon it. The ancient medicine men knew all about the rejuvenating qualities of garlic and onions. They knew about that secret ingredient, which lasted only for one hour in fresh onions, which would act like a human power-pack.

I am telling you this secret, as it was passed down to me by the elders. Fresh onion, not more than one hour old is capable of giving you more energy and improving your level of vitality and strength – physical and mental.

There are more than 325 varieties of onions, found all over the world. The pungent qualities of members of this particular family are because of the presence of sulfur in the bulbs. This is aromatic, and easily assimilated in the air, when you remove the papery cover of onions or garlic.

In the history of mankind, it has been said that Roman soldiers as well as the people building the great pyramids were fed onions as part of their daily meals, without which they would certainly rebel. Sickening workers – they were not slaves, they were free men helping in the building of these giant architectural wonders just to keep themselves occupied in times when the Nile was in flood – were given onion juice, in order to keep them disease-free.

Even today, there are plenty of hard labor workers in many impoverished parts of the world, who manage to survive on bread and onions.

Garlic

Garlic (*Allium sativum*) is a hardy perennial plant, native to southern Europe. Garlic differs from the onion in that instead of producing one large bulb, it is going produce a group of bulbs. These are called cloves. The cloves are covered with a thin skin. Garlic is a cross pollinated crop, which is usually propagated by these cloves.

Garlic enjoys growing in a somewhat moderate temperature, in summer and winter. Why not, because after all, its native land is never subjected to extremes of temperature.

You can also grow it as a cool season crop. Garlic plants are going to respond well to a longer day length. They are going to form bulbs under long days. This does not depend on the size of the plant.

You can also grow it at an elevation of 1000 – 1350 meters above sea level. All it asks is that the soil should be fertile and well-drained. It should also be loamy. Any soil on which you grow onions is going to be excellent for garlic. That means the soil is going to be medium black, rich in organic fertilizer and humus with a pH value of 6 – 7. Highly alkaline and saline soils are not conducive to good garlic growth.

The time of planting is early. Depending on the weather, you are going to start planting as early as May up to October in the plains. In the years, you can plant in March and April, and May and October.

The cloves are going to be placed with their growing end up words about 5 – 7.5 cm deep in the prepared soil. The soil is prepared beforehand with organic fertilizer added to it, a month before sowing. The planting distance can be 10 – 15 cm x 8 – 10 cm depending on the size of the cloves.

If you plant garlic in heavy clay soil, you are going to get misshapen bulbs. Harvesting is also going to be difficult.

Main popular varieties of garlic grown all over the world are "Early" and "Late." The late variety is going to have pinkish brown cloves. It matures 2 – 3 weeks later than the early variety. It is considered to be higher quality garlic, even though it yields lesser than the early variety.

The early variety has tan colored cloves. It is also a poor keeper in storage.

When you are planting garlic you separate the cloves and plant them with their growing ends up, as I said before, with about 800 pounds of cloves per hectare! But then, as I am planting them in a small bed, I am just going to use about 2 – 3 pounds of healthy juicy cloves.

Remember when you are planting –: any cloves, which are long and slender in the center should be discarded, because they are going to give poorly developed bulbs.

Long days and high temperatures, especially let us say in California, – where you are going to plant them from late October to January – is going to favor bulb development in a garlic plant.

As soon as the bulbing commences, you will see a fall in the leafy vegetation growth. That means if you want to get a higher yield, you must plant early enough so that a larger vegetative plant can develop under the short days, and cool temperatures.

The garlic yield potential of a plant is going to depend on the amount of vegetative growth made before bulbing commences. The optimum soil moisture for the better growth from cloves should be 80 – 90% of the field absorption capacity. That means that there should absolutely be no scarcity of water in the soil during the growing season. Otherwise, the development of the bulbs is going to be checked

Late plantings do not permit proper and adequate vegetative development of the plant. This means that you are going to get a lower yield.

Harvesting

The bulb is going to mature 120 – 180 days after planting, depending on the plant variety, climate, and the soil

The crop is going to be harvested when the tops are partly dry and begin to fall over. This is going to occur in June and July. The plants are going to be loosened by running a cutting bar or any other deep digging garden implement under the bulbs. These bulbs can now be pulled by hand and placed in small bunches in wind-rows.

These wind – rows are made with the tops up to facilitate the drying process. It also protects the bulbs from the sun. The plants are allowed to dry for one week or more in the field. After that the tops and the roots are going to be removed by hands or with shears.

The top is cut an inch above the bulb. The roots are trimmed about half an inch below the bulb. The bulbs are now going to be piled up again in the field, and covered with the tops so that they can be cured longer if you want it so.

When they are completely dry, you can grade them, and pack them in open mesh bags for storage in your own home, or for the market. In many places where garlic is still considered to be a gourmet food fit for only those people who have acquired its taste – believe it or not there are still some pockets of the world, where this is so – retail trade outlets are going to have one or 2 bulbs packed in small film bags or in small paper boxes with a film window.

Garlic is going to store well under a wider range of temperatures. However, it is going to sprout most quickly at temperatures near 40°. The humidity in the storage should be low at all times to discourage any sort of fungus and mold development as well as sprouting in the roots.

Garlic is usually used as a flavoring condiment and a flavoring for soups, pickles, stews and salads.

Herbs and onions and garlic…

Health Benefits of Garlic

According to Hippocrates, known as the father of Western medicine, good health, meant "let food be thy medicine and medicine be thy food."

That meant that he was heavily into naturopathic treatments, for curing ailments, all those millenniums ago.

Traditionally, garlic is known as the stinking Rose, because of its pungent smell. Funnily enough, Romans did not like the strong odor of garlic in their meals, and that is why they left garlic to the soldiers and to the laborers.

It is possible that since then, the prejudice against garlic as a lowly vegetable has persisted subconsciously and *garlic eater* is still a pejorative term in many parts of Europe, even though garlic is an important part of Italian cuisine today.

Garlic is definitely not just a spicy and pungent condiment and herb. It is chockablock full of nutritional and healthy properties.

Weight Loss through Garlic

That's so unfair. Greens and now maybe garlic?

Many people do not know that garlic is an excellent way to reduce weight. Eat a few cloves of garlic regularly and this is going to stimulate the digestive enzymes. This contributes to weight loss. It also reduces hunger pangs. That is because garlic is considered to be an appetite suppressant. This is the reason why garlic and onions were a major part of the ancient diet given to laborers and hard workers, so that they had plenty of energy to work, but they did not feel hungry.

Garlic is also able to improve your body's metabolism rate. This is because it is going to stimulate the nervous system to release more adrenalin. That means more calories are going to be burnt up. And that also means an automatic weight-loss.

Antiviral and Antibacterial

Garlic prevents sickness by boosting up your natural immunity system.

Since ancient times, garlic, and onions were considered to be the best antibacterial and antiviral herbs available to mankind. 21st-century research shows that fresh garlic juice is capable of fighting bacterial. That is because it has very powerful antibiotic properties.

It is also capable of controlling fungal and viral infections. If you suffering from frequent cough and colds, you may try this natural prevention. Take one teaspoonful of fresh garlic juice, mixed with one teaspoonful of fresh onion juice, every night before you go to sleep. You are soon going to find yourself with a stronger immunity system.

Also, you may find yourself suffering from throat irritations and respiratory tract infections in the winter. Garlic and onion juice, mixed together is capable of getting rid of this problem.

In ancient times, garlic was considered to be an important medicine to treat bronchitis.

Skin Protector

People who are suffering from acne, pimples or blemishes in the skin, or just want a glowing complexion just need to crush two cloves of raw garlic. Gulp them down every day with warm water early in the morning . This is considered to be an extremely good blood purifier. It is also going to get rid of any potential skin infections by cleansing your body internally.

When I was training students at the aviation school, they had a class where there was extensive personality grooming and training. Skin care, including meticulous cleansing, both for men and women was a part of this curriculum.

One fine day I was approached by one of my irate faculty colleagues. What had I done? What advice had I given one of the students? His perfect complexion was all shot to pieces. It was all raw and red.

When I calmed K. down because I was extremely bewildered at this unjustified accusation, I found out that that enterprising young youngster had crushed raw garlic and applied it all over his skin. There had been a tiny pimple outbreak, and he had decided to prevent this from spreading.[1]

Unfortunately, even a man's skin on the face is sensitive. So that garlic was enough to burn the tender surface. I had to cure the skin with honey and rosewater, but that was a signal lesson to all the rest of the students. After that, he had to cool the skin down even more with vinegar and cold milk. After a week or so, his skin was back to normal.

Do not experiment with herbs externally unless under the close supervision of an experienced naturalist!

---

[1] By the way, K did not apologize for biting off my head. Everybody knew that I was a herbalist and naturalist, so it was just possible that I had advised Jeffrey to do exactly that.

Whatever the Internet may say, do not apply raw garlic or garlic juice on your face.

Garlic for Your Liver

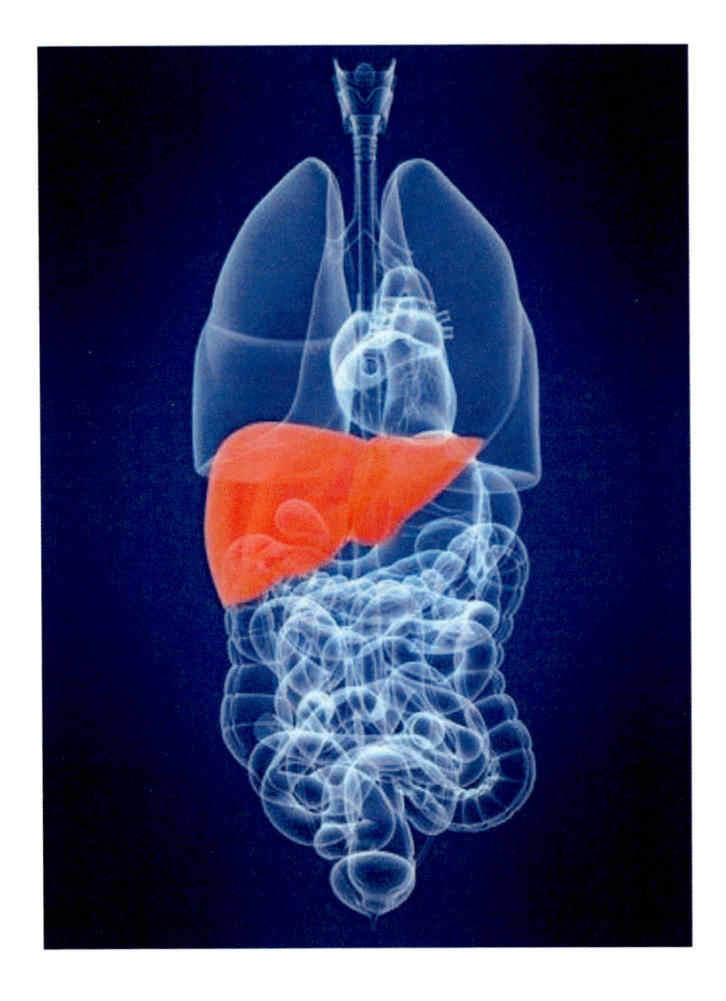

The same powerful Selenium and allicin, which is capable of burning tender skin, has a quite different effect when it is taken internally. It produces bile. This is a fluid produced by the liver to aid in the digestion process.

This means that anybody suffering from Fatty Liver Disease should increase their garlic intake. Also, garlic has antioxidant properties which are going to be the toxic substances filtered by your liver from reaching the other organs in your body.

Blood Sugar Reduction

If you are suffering from high blood sugar levels in your blood, you can try a little bit more of garlic in your diet. This is going to increase the amount of insulin, which is released in the body. It is also going to improve glucose tolerance. Crush two cloves of garlic and swallow them with a glass of warm water.

Cholesterol Reduction

Garlic reduces the chances of heart ailments.

Eating more garlic is going to help in reducing the bad cholesterol also known as LDL in your body by anywhere between 6 – 10%. It is possibly this particular reason why people in Mediterranean countries who eat large amounts of garlic suffered less from cholesterol and also plaque and deposits in the arteries.

Onions

According to archaeologists onions have been natives of Asia, perhaps from Palestine to the Indian subcontinent. It has been in cultivation and has been used as a food from the earliest periods of history. It has been mentioned in the Holy Bible as one of the foods for which the Israelites longed in the wilderness.

I can very well believe it, because any meal without onions in raw or cooked form seems a bit incomplete, especially for a person who has been spoiled that way.

Allium Cepa is grown all over the world, as a cool season crop, but can also be grown in a wide range of climatic conditions.

As long as there is no extreme heat and cold, you can grow onions to your heart's delight. However, they do not enjoy a very heavy rainfall either. You can grow onions as a summer crop, if the annual rainfall in your area is not more than 70 – 100 centimeters, especially in rainy weather.

The best temperature for growing onions is 12 – 21°C before they start bulbing. The best bulb development is ideal at 15 – 25°C. You may find your plants growing leggy and "bolting", if the temperature is very low in the early stages of the plant development.

Many of the Native American species, growing wild are going to produce bulbils instead of seed in the flower cluster.

Soil Preparation for Onions

Onions can be grown on nearly all types of soils, from sandy loams, and even black, heavy clay soil, especially one which is full of humus. However it likes sandy soil and loose loam the best. Proper drainage and sufficient organic matter is necessary for a high yield. The ideal pH of soil is 5.7 – 6.6.

However, it is not going to grow in alkaline soil or marshy soil. The greatest difficulty encountered in growing onions on clay soil is that the tendency of this soil is to run together and bake after a hard rain.

This is going to be injurious after the seed has been sown and before the plants have attained a sufficient size to permit proper cultivation.

Sandy loam soil, which has plenty of humus in it and is heavily fertilized with organic manure is the best choice of soil. In fact, if you have soil with plenty of compost in it, just sow your onion bulbs in it, and wait to harvest a really rich crop. Of course you need proper drainage, because any bulb plant is definitely not going to grow properly, if it has to grow in water, which does not drain away.

Prepare the soil for onions, properly by pulverizing the soil. It should have a smooth surface. You can drag or roll the land just before planting.

Organic manure is added to the soil before you plant the onions, especially it has not been rotted well. That is because fresh manure is going to have weed seeds. Unless you plough this manure under, it is going to interfere with the planting and the cultivating.

If you are growing onions in a big way, you can apply 15 – 20 tons of organic manure per acre. Farm produce is best.

This fresh organic fertilizer should be turned over in the fall or you can turn it as early in the spring us as possible. This fertilizer can either be broadcast, you can drill it in before planting as it has been done traditionally down the ages.

Seed Propagation

Onions are propagated by seed sown when the crops are to mature. This is done by raising the seedlings and transplanting them in the field. The seedlings can be raised in a greenhouse hotbed or outdoor seedbed.

For the production of seedlings, you are going to sow the seed in outdoor seedbeds 6 – 10 weeks before you intend to transplant them in the field.

Seed sowing is going to be done, depending on your location from March to April in hilly areas, and August to November in the plains.

If you want green onions for salads in early winter, you can place bulbs at 15 cm on the sides of ridges 15 cm wide or in beds. You can also cultivate onions through direct seeding. Seed 5 pounds in mid January – February, depending on the weather in an area about 200 m long.

About 10 – 12 pounds of seeds are going to give you enough of seedlings for planting in a 1 half acre area.

Planting

The best time for planting is going to depend on the locality, the type of onions and the method of propagation which you are using. If you want to plant bulbs you are going to plant them as early in the spring, as you can prepare the soil. This is so that any sort of light freeze does not injure them.

When you are using seedlings, try planting them in the fall.

When you are planting the seeds, where you intend the crop to mature, you can sow them as early as possible after the frosts are over in the spring. This is done where severe frost occurs.

Planting of the seedlings is done mainly by the hand, and you are going to space the plants 3 – 4 inches apart in 14 – 16 inches apart rows.

It has been seen that spacing the transplants more than 2 – 3 inches apart in the row is going to result in an increase in the size of the bulbs. It is also going to show a decrease in the yield per acre.

Early planting is important in all the regions of the earth, where the crop is grown during the long warm days of summer. As the bulbing is controlled by the length of the day and the temperature, the plants are going to form bulbs at about the same time regardless of when they are planted.

Leaf initiation and growth is going to stop than the bulbing starts. The growth of the bulb is going to depend on the leaves, which are already present when the bulbing commences.

Early planting is going to result in higher yield. This is because it permits more leaves to develop before the bulbing starts than in the case of later planting.

Methods of planting has not changed down the ages. seeds are normally sown with a drill when the crop is grown commercially. 4 – 6 pounds of seed is used to the acre, if it is sown where the onions are to mature.

Thinning

The practice of sowing onion seeds thickly and then thinning the seedlings to the desired distance has been in vogue for centuries. However, nowadays, the tendency is to sow the seed more thinly and dispense with thinning because this is quite an expensive operation. However, you can get a larger yield, when you grow the onions thickly, because large sizes are of no importance for these onions and in such cases thinning is not justified.

Proper cultivation of Onions

To produce a good crop of onions it is necessary that you keep the weeds under control. Hand de – weeding is thus necessary. This is of special importance during the early growth of onions as the plant is going to grow slowly at first. This is a time when it is most vulnerable to weeds.

Cultivation of the onion is going to begin as soon as the plants appear above the surface of the soil. It is going to continue until the tops begin to interfere with the cultivation work.

If you have onions growing on a larger area, you can look at other de-weeding tools, especially small garden tractors. These are special models of regular farm tractors, and are used for closely spaced crops. Borrow one; do not buy one, unless you intend to make a living from growing and selling onions.

Once upon a time, farmers used to use wheel hoes for de-weeding.

You may want to see this interesting URL about this environment friendly gardening tool.

https://www.youtube.com/watch?v=MUwSmojsUxY

Harvesting

Onions for use in the green stage are harvested as soon as they reach edibles size. The plants are pulled by hand. The roots are going to be trimmed. The outside skin is going to be peeled off thus leaving the stem clean and white.

These onions are now going to be washed and sorted out. They are then going to be tied in bunches. The size of the bunch is going to depend on your preference are the local market preferences.

If you leave them in the ground until the tops are dead, the bulbs are going to develop roots. This is going to result in reducing the market value of the onions.

In many parts of the world, harvesting is delayed until most of the tops are broken over. However, it is sensible to pull the onion crop and throw them into wind –rows [a wind row is a long row of cut harvest, which is allowed to stay in the field, and dry, until it is collected and bunched up.] and allow them to dry before you top them. Nowadays, most of these crops are harvested by machines that remove the bulbs from the soil and cut off the tops.

When you are pulling them by hand, you should place them in the windrows in such a manner that the tops partly cover the bulbs. This is to prevent them from suffering from sunburn- sunscald.

These are usually left in the windrows long enough for the tops to become dry. The length of time required is going to depend on the weather. It can be anywhere between 3 – 10 or more days.

To Top or Not to Top

This is a matter which is still being discussed warmly by gardeners, who have left their harvest in windrows in order to dry.

It has been seen that onion bulbs are going to lose weight during the curing in the windrows whether or not they are topped, but more weight is going to be lost during the first few days *when the tops are left intact.*

Also, it has been proven that bulbs with the tops intact are going to have much higher percentage of dry matter after curing than bulbs with the tops chopped off.

This difference may be due to greater loss of water from the bulbs with the foliage intact. It can also be possible because of movement of the materials from the tops to the bulbs.

After the tops have been dry down, they are going to be cut off by hand with shears or with a knife. Remember to leave ½ – 1 inch of the tops attached to the bulb. If they are cut too close, the neck is not going to close well and decay organisms are going to thus have easy access to the bulb.

Storage

Onions should be well ripened and thoroughly dry before they are stored. This curing process is normally done in the field or in a shed, where they are going to be kept for 3 – 4 weeks. Immature, soft and thick necked bulbs should be used up or send to the market, as soon as you harvest them. Do not store them.

Proper storage of onions include good ventilation, low-temperature, dry atmosphere and protection against freezing.

Chives

Chive- *Allium Schoenopraesum*-is a perennial, possibly a native of Europe. It is a popular plant in home gardens. But it is not grown to any great extent for marketing purposes unless you have a cottage cheese manufacturing industry right in your city, where you are going to get chive flavored products on your store shelves.

The plant is going to grow in thick tufts. It produces very small oval bulbs, forming a compact mass. It has attractive lavender flowers, which in part accounts for its popularity among home gardeners.

It is propagated by seed and by division of the tufts. Although the plant is a perennial, it is a good plan to take up the clumps and replant them every 2 or 3 years.

If you want a larger harvest, I would suggest that you sow the seed in the spring. The whole onion family seed sowing process is the same, which is previously discussed in detail under the topic "Onions" above.

The chive is grown for its leaves. These are cut by hand with a knife. This cutting is going to stimulate further growth. Farmers in Europe and on Long Island pick up the clumps in the fall. These are then potted in paper pots or strawberry packing boxes. They are then placed in a cold frame.

Some of the plants are going to be placed in a warm greenhouse for 2 or 3 weeks at intervals. They are then going to be sold as potted plants.

These pots are going to supply you with fresh chives for a period of several weeks if you take good care of them.

Chives are used as a seasoning in salads, chopped up in omelettes, and in other dishes. However, most of the product is sold by market gardeners to processors where the finely chopped leaves are going to be mixed up with cottage cheese or cream cheese and sold in the retail market.

So where are the potted chives?

Shallots

Shallots *(Allium ascalonicum)* are supposed to be natives of Western Asia. They are perennial plants and seldom produce seeds, but the bulb when planted can divide into a number of cloves.

Growing Shallots

Shallots have been in cultivation since the dawn of time. They are sometimes grown for the dry bulbs, but usually for the younger plants which are normally used in the same way as one would use green onions.

In some parts of the world, the word *shallots* is used for any green onions, including leeks and spring onions. This is known as a winter crop, for a bunch of green, but when it is grown as a summer of, it is used for its dry bulbs.

More than 5600 acres of ground in Louisiana have been bearing a cash crop of shallots valued at 1, 600, 000 dollars! And here was I just under the impression that these were simple younger cousins of the onion!

The variety which is grown here is called Louisiana, Pearl. This is tolerant to diseases like pink root. Some plantings are made here in August, although the bulk of the crop is planted during October, with the later plantings until January. Naturally, you are going to be taking the advice of your neighborhood nursery market gardener, or checking time almanacs on the Internet to see other planting times, depending on your location.

But do not worry; shallots are able to grow in any sort of soil, anywhere in the world where you have plenty of sun and plenty of water.

The dry bulb is going to be planted in soil mounds six – eight inches apart. One large bulb or two small bulbs can be planted in each mound.

The rows are three – six feet apart. They are ridged to ensure proper drainage.

Cover the bulbs up with about half an inch of soil. This shallow cultivation is made because then you can do proper weed control. This weed control is going to be done about five weeks before your plants are ready for harvest. Two inches of soil is now going to be banked around the plants.

Two weeks later, you can add another two inches. This is so that the blanched portion of the shallots can be about 2 ½ inches in length.

Harvest

Harvesting is normally done in November, and ends in May. That is done quite easily by pulling out the shallots by hand after they have obtained a diameter of at least ¼ of an inch.

The outer skin is going to be peeled off and the roots are going to be trimmed. Then you can wash them, bunch them and pack them for market, or eat them for lunch or dinner.

Commercially barrels containing 20 dozen bunches have been the standard shallot containers for many years, arriving in the market gardens. They are also packed in one bushel or 1 1/3 bushel crates. These are capable of folding five – eight dozen bunches.

Shallots are preserved by packing them with crushed ice, so that they do not heat and spoil rapidly. The ice is going to prevent this spoilage.

Growing shallots for Bulbs

If you are growing shallots for dry bulbs, you are going to get a better yield, at higher temperatures. Plants grown at temperatures of 70 degrees Fahrenheit and higher are going to form bulbs larger bulbs can also be produced in areas, where you have about 15 hours of sun than in areas where you have around 10 hours of sun.

When the temperature is lower than 70 degrees Fahrenheit, you are not going to get bulbs, regardless of the length of the day.

For maximum yield of dry bulbs, they should be planted early in the spring so that they can get a large amount of vegetative growth before the bulbing process commences.

Individual bulbs should be about one inch in diameter. They are going to have a more delicate flavor than onions do. Many people have stopped growing dry bulbs for the market, because greens of shallots are much more in demand.

Use these shallot greens to flavor soups and as an accompaniment to meat dishes. If you cannot bear the thought of onion breath, eat shallots and get about the same amount of nutrition and benefits, and which you are going to expect from a plant belonging to the allium family.

Leeks

Leeks [*Allium Porrum*] is a biennial plant, grown for its blanched leaves and stem. Leeks originated in the Mediterranean region, where they have been in cultivation since prehistoric times.

The ancient Greeks and Romans could not do without leeks in their cuisine. Even though the demand for market growers to grow leeks, for city consumption is increasing yearly, leeks are still not as popular as onions, and even shallots as greens.

This is a plant which does not form bulbs. You can consume it raw. You can add it in salads. You can cook it in soups and stews to impart a delicious delicate flavor to the pottage.

Leek Propagation

Leeks are propagated entirely from seed. These can be sown in a greenhouse, nursery or hotbed from the end of September – October. The young plants are going to be transplanted in the garden in trenches about 40 centimeters deep.

Plant the seedlings, at 15 centimeters on the side of 50 centimeter wide ridges. You are going to blanch the plants by banking them with soil. This blanking is going to be done slowly as the plants grow.

Do not start this process too early, when the plants are still young. This banking is going to be done gradually, while they are growing. If you do that when they are still very young, they are going to start rotting.

Leek plants are going to be larger than onions. You can market them in bunches, just like you do Shallots and green onions.

Conclusion

This book gives you plenty of information about the allium family and how you can grow them in your garden. These herbs have been an integral part of human life for millenniums. To make onions more popular in France, especially in the 17 century, royalty decided on a great exercise of snobbery. Only aristocrats and royalty could wear onion flowers on their buttonholes.

The common people decided that there was something special about these pungent smelling bulbs, and that is why they began to look for Ways and Means in which they could get access to these plants.

And because it was supposedly inaccessible, just like the potato, – which incidentally was also popularized by the same result for royalty only edict – onions have now become a major part of French cuisine.

So, started growing these plants in your garden, and get them fresh.

Live Long and Prosper!

Author Bio

Dueep Jyot Singh is a Management and IT Professional who managed to gather Postgraduate qualifications in Management and English and Degrees in Science, French and Education while pursuing different enjoyable career options like being an hospital administrator, IT,SEO and HRD Database Manager/ trainer, movie , radio and TV scriptwriter, theatre artiste and public speaker, lecturer in French, Marketing and Advertising, ex-Editor of Hearts On Fire (now known as Solstice) Books Missouri USA, advice columnist and cartoonist, publisher and Aviation School trainer, ex-moderator on Medico.in, banker, student councilor ,travelogue writer … among other things!

One fine morning, she decided that she had enough of killing herself by Degrees and went back to her first love -- writing. It's more enjoyable! She already has 48 published academic and 14 fiction- in- different- genre books under her belt.

When she is not designing websites or making Graphic design illustrations for clients , she is browsing through old bookshops hunting for treasures, of which she has an enviable collection – including R.L. Stevenson, O.Henry, Dornford Yates, Maurice Walsh, De Maupassant, Victor Hugo, Sapper, C.N. Williamson, "Bartimeus" and the crown of her collection- Dickens "The Old Curiosity Shop," and "Martin Chuzzlewit" and so on… Just call her "Renaissance Woman") - collecting herbal remedies, acting like Universal Helping Hand/Agony Aunt, or escaping to her dear mountains for a bit of exploring, collecting herbs and plants and trekking.

Check out some of the other JD-Biz Publishing books

[Gardening Series on Amazon](https://amazon.com)

Health Learning Series

Country Life Books

GRANDMA'S
NATURAL REMEDIES
AND ANCIENT HERBAL
BEAUTY RECIPES
Volume 1
HEALTH LEARNING SERIES
DUEEP J SINGH AND J DAVIDSON
GRANDMA'S
NATURAL REMEDIES
AND ANCIENT HERBAL
BEAUTY RECIPES
Volume 2
HEALTH LEARNING SERIES
DUEEP J SINGH AND J DAVIDSON
GRANDMA'S
NATURAL REMEDIES
AND ANCIENT RECIPES
GRANDMA'S CURE FOR OBESITY
GRANDMA'S CURE FOR THE COMMON COLD
Volume 3
HEALTH LEARNING SERIES
DUEEP J SINGH AND J DAVIDSON
GRANDMA'S
NATURAL REMEDIES AND
ANCIENT HERBAL RECIPES
Volume 4
HEALTH LEARNING SERIES
DUEEP J SINGH AND J DAVIDSON
GRANDMA'S
HERBAL LORE
ANCIENT HERBAL RECIPES AND REMEDIES
Volume 5
HEALTH LEARNING SERIES
DUEEP J SINGH AND J DAVIDSON
GRANDMA'S
ANCIENT
BEAUTY REMEDIES
FROM HER KITCHEN
Volume 6
HEALTH LEARNING SERIES
DUEEP J SINGH AND J DAVIDSON
GRANDMA'S
EASY TO USE TIPS
IN THE KITCHEN AND OUTDOORS
Volume 7
HEALTH LEARNING SERIES
DUEEP J SINGH AND J DAVIDSON
GRANDMA'S
HOUSEHOLD HINTS AND RECIPES
USING TIME TESTED
ECONOMICAL TIPS IN YOUR HOME
75 Tips
Remove Stains
Peel Tomatoes
Perfect Pies
HEALTH LEARNING SERIES
DUEEP J SINGH AND J DAVIDSON
GRANDMA'S
NATURAL REMEDIES
AND ANCIENT RECIPES
ALL 5 BOOKS IN 1
HEALTH LEARNING SERIES
DUEEP J SINGH AND J DAVIDSON

Health Learning Series

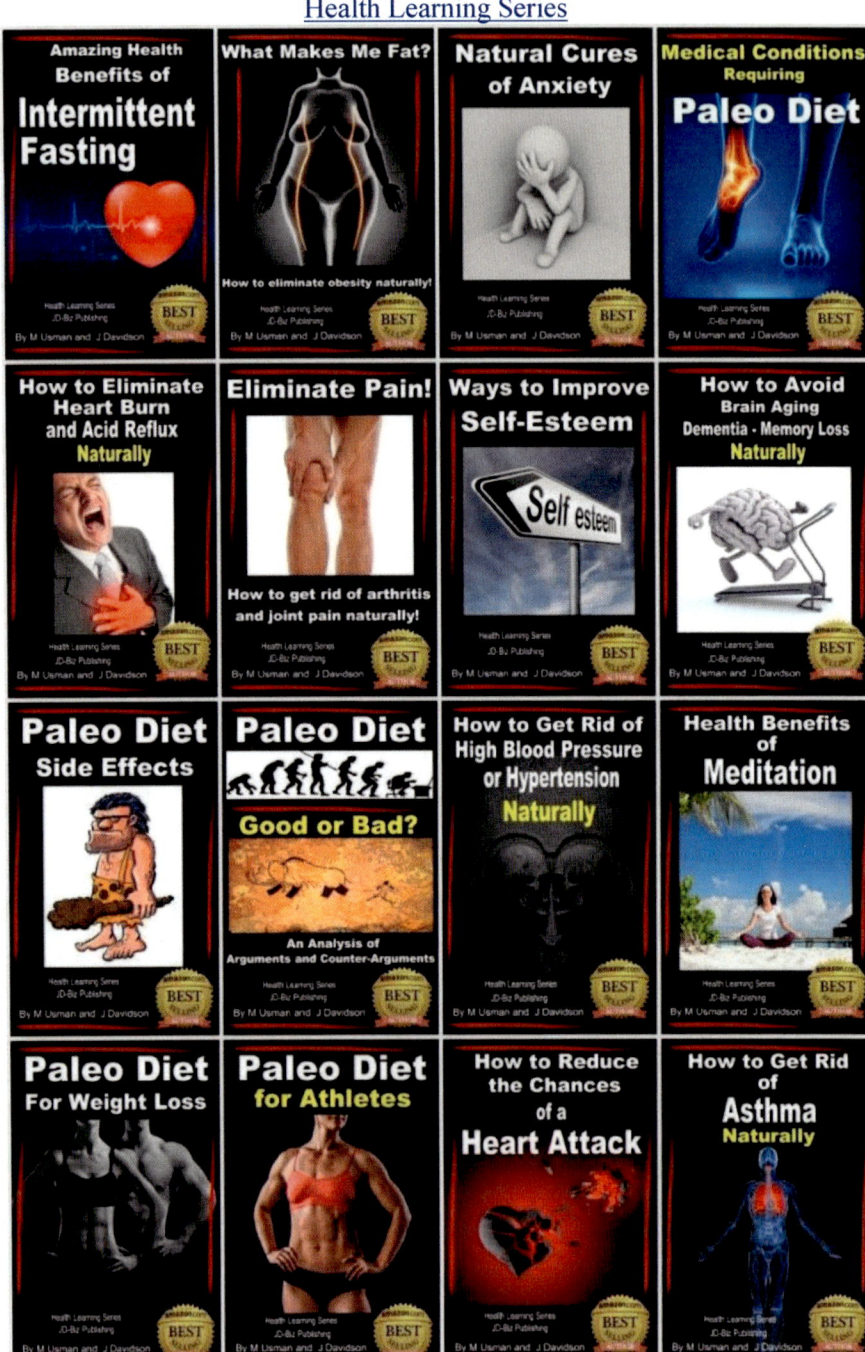

Amazing Animal Book Series

Introduction to The Onion Family   Page 57

Learn To Draw Series

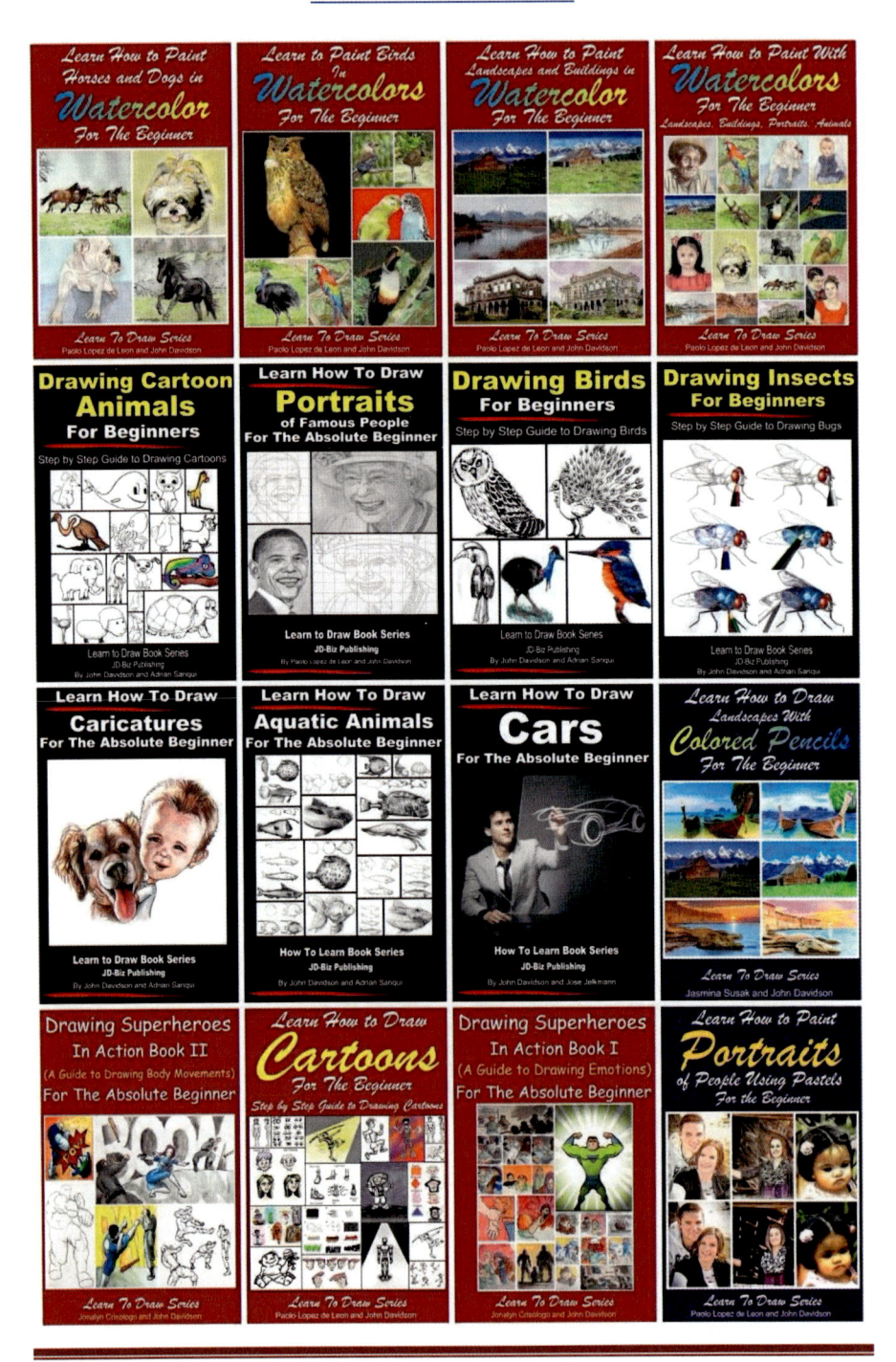

Introduction to The Onion Family   Page 58

How to Build and Plan Books

Introduction to The Onion Family

Entrepreneur Book Series

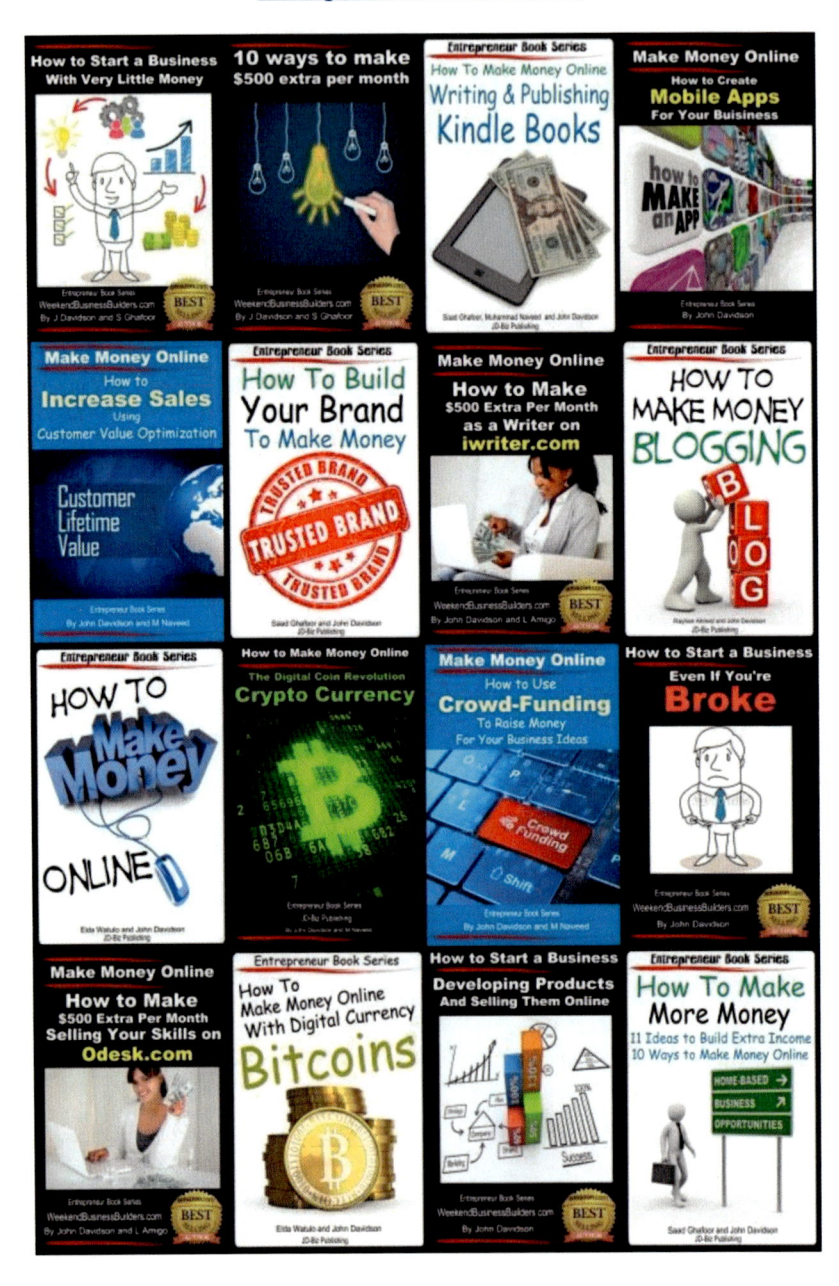

Our books are available at

1. Amazon.com
2. Barnes and Noble
3. Itunes
4. Kobo
5. Smashwords
6. Google Play Books

Publisher

JD-Biz Corp

P O Box 374

Mendon, Utah 84325

http://www.jd-biz.com/

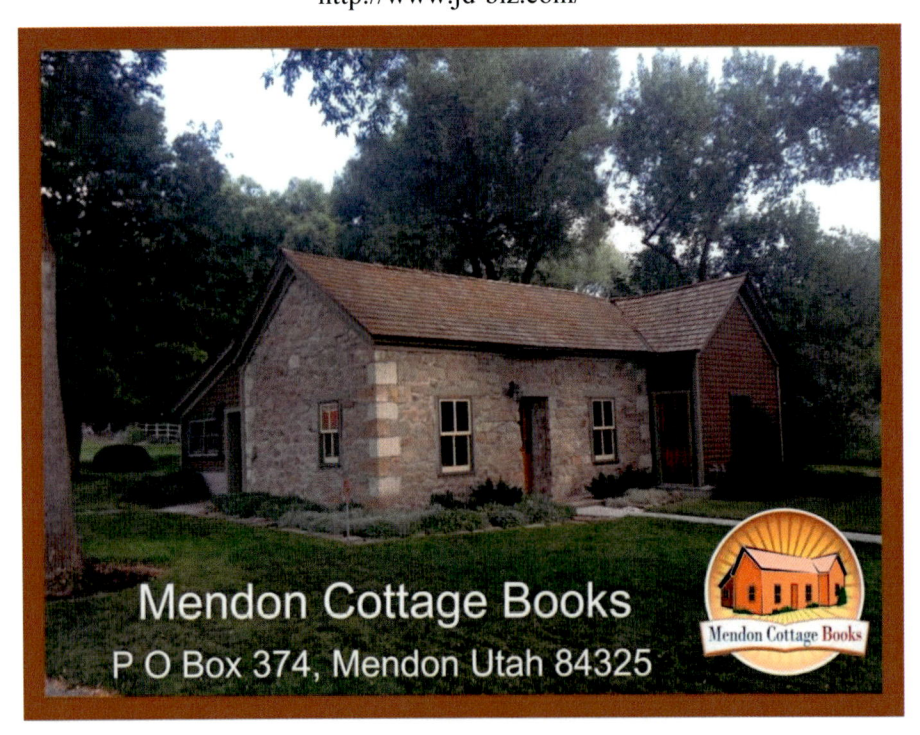

Made in the USA
Las Vegas, NV
13 January 2022